WOMBAT

By Colleen Sexton

Consultant: Darin Collins, DVM
Director, Animal Health Programs, Woodland Park Zoo

BEARPORT
PUBLISHING

Minneapolis, Minnesota

Credits

cover, © Martin Pelanek/Shutterstock, © MikeMakarenko/Shutterstock, and © Sandra Caldwell/Shutterstock; 3, © Hayley Roberts Photo/Shutterstock; 4, 5, © Dave Watts/Alamy Stock Photo; 6, © Jason Pratt/Wikipedia; 6, © Eva Hejda/Wikipedia; 7, © Juergen & Christine Sohns/Minden Pictures; 8, © David Whidborne/Shutterstock; 9, © ozflash/iStock; 10, © Sonijya/Shutterstock; 11, © anthony pilling/Alamy Stock Photo; 12, © Pixelheld/Shutterstock; 13, © Biosphoto/Biosphoto; 15, © Michael R Evans/Shutterstock; 16, © Sonijya/Shutterstock; 17, © Andreas Ruhz/Shutterstock; 18, © NHPA/NHPA; 19, © Colin Munro/Alamy Stock Photo; 21, © R.J. Low/Shutterstock; 23, © Picture Partners/Alamy Stock Photo

President: Jen Jenson
Director of Product Development: Spencer Brinker
Editor: Allison Juda
Designer: Micah Edel

Library of Congress Cataloging-in-Publication Data

Names: Sexton, Colleen A., 1967- author.
Title: Wombat / Colleen Sexton.
Description: Minneapolis, Minnesota : Bearport Publishing Company, [2021] |
   Series: Library of awesome animals | Includes bibliographical references and index.
Identifiers: LCCN 2020014036 (print) | LCCN 2020014037 (ebook) |
   ISBN 9781647471491 (library binding) | ISBN 9781647471606 (paperback) | ISBN 9781647471712 (ebook)
Subjects: LCSH: Wombats—Juvenile literature.
Classification: LCC QL737.M39 S49 2021 (print) | LCC QL737.M39 (ebook) | DDC 599.2/4—dc23
LC record available at https://lccn.loc.gov/2020014036
LC ebook record available at https://lccn.loc.gov/2020014037

For more information, write to Bearport Publishing, 5357 Penn Avenue South, Minneapolis, MN 55419.
Printed in the United States of America.

Contents

Awesome Wombats! 4

Three of a Kind 6

Built for Digging 8

Going Underground 10

Great Grazing 12

It Comes with the Territory 14

Buns of Steel 16

Baby Wombats 18

Growing Up 20

Information Station 22
Glossary 23
Index 24
Read More 24
Learn More Online 24
About the Author 24

AWESOME
Wombats!

POP! Two wombats poke their heads out of a **burrow**. It's time for the nightly search for food. At home in a burrow or **grazing** under starry skies, wombats are awesome!

WOMBATS ARE **NOCTURNAL** ANIMALS.
THEY ARE ACTIVE MOSTLY AT NIGHT.

Three of a Kind

Three types of wombats live in the forests and grasslands of Australia. Common, or bare-nosed, wombats have brown fur, round ears, and bare noses. Northern hairy-nosed wombats and southern hairy-nosed wombats have (you guessed it!) hairy noses. They also have gray fur and pointy ears.

A northern
hairy-nosed wombat

A southern
hairy-nosed wombat

A bare-nosed wombat

MOST OF THE WOMBATS IN AUSTRALIA ARE BARE-NOSED WOMBATS.

7

Built for Digging

The wombat has a strong neck and shoulders. Short, powerful legs end with wide feet and sharp claws that are perfect for digging. The wombat digs a burrow with one front foot at a time. It digs for a while and then switches to the other foot. *SNIP!* It bites through roots that are in the way.

A wombat claw

8

Going Underground

A wombat has many underground burrows. Its main burrow has several entrances that lead to a series of tunnels and rooms. Sometimes, a wombat lines its sleeping room with dried grasses, leaves, bark, and twigs.

Wombats will also dig short burrows to use for a quick rest or as a place to hide. They spend about two-thirds of their lives underground.

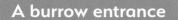

A burrow entrance

LIVING UNDERGROUND HELPS WOMBATS STAY COOL DURING HOT WEATHER AND WARM DURING COLD WEATHER.

Great Grazing

The wombat leaves its burrow to eat. It spends three to eight hours every night grazing on grasses and nibbling on roots. **MUNCH!** Eating wears down the wombat's strong teeth, which never stop growing.

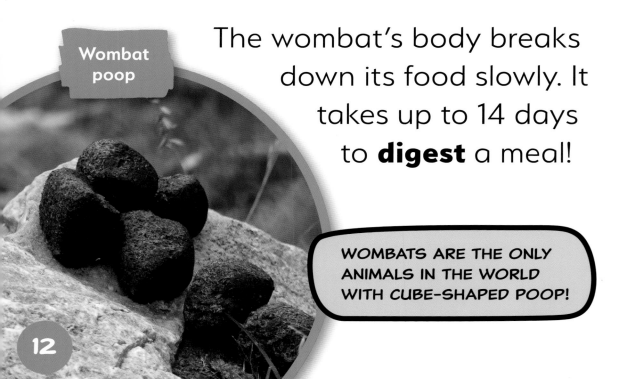

Wombat poop

The wombat's body breaks down its food slowly. It takes up to 14 days to **digest** a meal!

WOMBATS ARE THE ONLY ANIMALS IN THE WORLD WITH CUBE-SHAPED POOP!

It Comes with the Territory

Hairy-nosed wombats often live together in a **colony**. But the bare-nosed wombat has its own space. It marks its **territory** to keep other wombats away.

CHICKER-CHICKER! CHUR! The wombat warns another wombat that has entered its territory. The other wombat needs to leave. It may be chased away if it comes closer.

THE WOMBAT USUALLY MOVES SLOWLY. BUT IT CAN RUN UP TO 25 MILES PER HOUR (40 KPH) IN SHORT BURSTS.

Buns of Steel

If a wild dog, fox, or other **predator** enters the wombat's territory, the furry digger scrambles into its nearest burrow. The wombat keeps its backside toward an attacker. With strong bones and thick skin, a wombat rump is hard to hurt.

A predator that follows a wombat into its burrow is in for a surprise. The wombat uses its rear to crush the attacker.

A wombat with its butt out

IF A WOMBAT CANNOT MAKE IT TO A BURROW, IT FIGHTS BY SCRATCHING WITH ITS CLAWS AND STABBING WITH ITS TEETH.

Baby Wombats

Once a year, bare-nosed wombats come together to **mate**. A female wombat makes her way to a male's territory. The female gives birth 21 to 30 days after they mate. The tiny baby is called a joey. It is about the size of a jellybean when it is born. The joey crawls into the pouch on its mother's belly.

A joey

THE WOMBAT'S POUCH OPENS TOWARD HER BACKSIDE. SHE CAN DIG A BURROW WITHOUT GETTING DIRT IN THE POUCH!

A joey in a pouch

Growing Up

The mother wombat's pouch has everything a joey needs. There, the joey drinks milk from its mother's body and stays warm and safe as it grows. The joey leaves the pouch for the first time when it is about five months old. By the time it is three years old, the wombat is ready to have its own young.

YOUNG WOMBATS PLAY! THEY RUN, JUMP IN THE AIR, TOSS THEIR HEADS FROM SIDE TO SIDE, AND ROLL DOWN HILLS.

WOMBATS ARE AWESOME!
LET'S LEARN EVEN MORE ABOUT THEM.

Kind of animal: Wombats are mammals. Most mammals have fur, give birth to live young, and drink milk from their mothers as babies.

Size: Wombats range in size from 28 to 47 inches (71 to 119 cm) long. That's about as big as a medium-sized dog.

Other marsupials: Mammals that carry their young in a pouch are called **marsupials** (mahr-SOO-pee-uhls). Wombats, kangaroos, and koalas are all marsupials.

WOMBATS AROUND THE WORLD

Indian Ocean

☐ WHERE WOMBATS LIVE

AUSTRALIA

Pacific Ocean

N
W E
S

Arctic Ocean

NORTH AMERICA   EUROPE   ASIA

Atlantic Ocean

Pacific Ocean

AFRICA

Indian Ocean

Pacific Ocean

SOUTH AMERICA

AUSTRALIA

Southern Ocean

ANTARCTICA

Glossary

burrow a hole or tunnel in the ground used by animals to live in

colony a group of animals that shares a home

digest to break down food to be used by the body

grazing eating grasses

marsupials animals that carry young in a pouch on their bodies

mate to come together to have young

nocturnal active mainly at night

predator an animal that hunts and kills other animals for food

territory the area where an animal lives

underground below the surface of the earth

Index

backside 16, 19
body 12, 20
burrow 4, 8–10, 12, 16–17, 19
digging 8, 10, 12, 16, 18
food 4, 12
fur 6

mate 18
pouch 18–20
predators 16
teeth 12, 17
territory 14, 16, 18
young 20

Read More

Fishman, Jon M. *Meet a Baby Wombat (Lightning Bolt Books. Baby Australian Animals)*. Minneapolis: Lerner Publications (2017).

Kenah, Katharine. *Super Marsupials: Kangaroos, Koalas, Wombats, and More (Let's-Read-and-Find-Out Science Level 1)*. New York: Harper (2019).

Learn More Online

1. Go to **www.factsurfer.com**
2. Enter "**Wombat**" into the search box.
3. Click on the cover of this book to see a list of websites.

About the Author

Colleen Sexton is a writer and editor. She is the author of more than 100 nonfiction books for kids on topics ranging from astronauts to glaciers to sharks. She lives in Minnesota.